GUANYIN: A MASTERPIECE REVEALED

GUANYIN
A Masterpiece Revealed

John Larson
& Rose Kerr

Victoria and Albert Museum

Published by the Victoria and Albert Museum, 1985
ISBN 0 905209 91 5

Designed by Paul Sharp
Printed by Lund Humphries
Bradford and London

Photography by John Hammond,
Ian Thomas, Steve Williams and Hugh Sainsbury

Analysis by Josephine Darrah, Ashok Roy,
Raymond White

Frontispiece
Fig 4 Guanyin, Victoria and Albert Museum (A.7.1935)
12th century Chinese, Jin Dynasty. H 96.4 cm
The sculpture before conservation in 1978

Contents

Fig 1 Bodhisattva, Jin dynasty, late
12th–early 13th century. Courtesy of the
Nelson Gallery of Art, Kansas City.

Introduction

Our carved wooden image of the Bodhisattva Guanyin (Jin period 1115–1234) sits in the posture of Royal Ease on a rocky throne. His elegant attitude of unconstrained nonchalance is a variation of the posture known in Indian iconography as *Mahārājalīlāsana*, and indicates the princely, worldly character of the Bodhisattva. The rocky base was probably formerly complemented by rock-like carvings up the sides of the niche and overhead. Thus, during the late twelfth century when Guanyin resided in a temple, he was sitting inside a grotto. For this statue represents the Bodhisattva in one of his most favoured aspects 'Guanyin of the Southern Seas', seated comfortably in a weathered grotto on the boulder-strewn shores of his island home, Putuo shan (off the coast of Zhejiang province, in eastern China).

Although invested with the magnificent trappings of the Bodhisattva, the figure is modelled after a recognisable human type. It has none of the exaggerated characteristics of the mightier Buddhist images. Slim but stocky, Guanyin corresponds to a typical Chinese body type: long in the torso and short in the leg, having small, broad feet with high arches, and plump hands with tapering fingers. These features, and those of the lovingly carved face, reflect a physical beauty somewhat alien to western taste. We are accustomed to portraying our gods and heroes in the classical mould; tall, broad-shouldered and muscular, with aquiline nose and penetrating gaze. Guanyin's fleshiness and faint air of femininity may puzzle those unacquainted with the male hero in Chinese drama and art.

His face is broad, with heavy-lidded eyes and pouting mouth under a full upper lip. The eyebrows are arched beneath a prominent brow, while the folds of flesh in the neck characterise both his human and his deified sublimity. He wears a *dhotī*, which is folded over at the waist and tied with a sash to form a double skirt, falling in a series of graceful folds to the feet. The Brahmanic cord is tied around his body, while a long scarf is draped over the left shoulder leaving the right shoulder bare. The princely jewels of the Bodhisattva are apparent; on his head the five-pointed crown, round the neck the necklet with *vajra* symbol, on his arms armlets and bracelets, while round the left ankle an anklet may just be glimpsed beneath the hem of his skirt. He wears earrings in his pendant lobes, and a crystal is embedded in the *ūrṇā* in the centre of his forehead.

Perhaps the most elaborately modelled section of the body is the head. Guanyin's hair is drawn up and tied in a high chignon on top of his head, against which the coronet rests. The coronet contains a standing figure of the Buddha Amitābha, and is tied round the head with a ribbon. Two loops of hair are swept round the ears, while a long strand of hair is allowed to fall to each shoulder. Rippling tendrils of hair flow down over his shoulders, their rhythm echoed in the folds of *dhotī* and scarf draped over the throne.

Although the sculpture is compact, it has a quality of dignity and grace. Seated at a slight angle, with the full weight of the body resting on the left arm, the figure is completely at ease. Relaxed and yet upright, the composition is harmonious from any angle. The off-centre pose is balanced by the squareness of the statue, and the tension in the squared angles of the limbs softened by flowing drapery.

So far the statue has been considered as a work of art, but we should never forget that Guanyin is a religious image. The cast of face with inward-turning gaze emphasises the Bodhisattva's powers as a comforter of men, while the corporeal character of body and dress stress his nearness and accessibility. Countless supplicants must have travelled to worship at his feet. If you have the time, take a moment to stand before the Bodhisattva, and allow yourself to become slowly aware of his serene beauty and power.

★   ★   ★

The Chinese Bodhisattva Guanyin is the same deity as the Indian Bodhisattva Avālokiteśvara. The Indian name for the deity consists of two parts, the *avalokita* participle meaning 'seen' and *lokeśvara* meaning 'lord'. The combination has been variously translated as 'the lord who sees' or 'the lord who is seen', but in either case the concept of accessibility and of the deity's presence in the world is established. A Tibetan translation of the name is 'He who casts his eye around' stressing the comforting power of the Bodhisattva to keep a benevolent eye on everything that goes on in the world, and to understand intuitively all these things. The Chinese name for the deity is Guanshiyin, which literally translated means 'one who hears the sounds (or prayers) of the world'. The abbreviated form, Guanyin 'one who hears sounds' is general, and the sense of the term close to that of the Indian original.

The Bodhisattva is one who has attained, or made the vow to attain, enlightenment and is thus entitled to enter *nirvāṇa*. He thereby escapes the worldly existence of craving and ignorance, as conceived in the Buddhist idea of perpetual re-birth. Although freed from the need to return to this existence, the Bodhisattvas chose to remain among men in order to help other mortals reach *nirvāṇa*. Avālokiteśvara is one of the most important Bodhisattvas, for he embodies compassion, a quality with basic appeal for the mass of Buddhist followers in both India and China.

Guanyin's appearance in Chinese Buddhism stems from two important sutras, both of which gained wide recognition. In the *Lotus sutra*, the deity is clearly identified as one with a merciful disposition. In the *Pure*

Land sutra, Guanyin is identified as one of the attendants and counsellor-emissaries to the Buddha Amitābha who presides over the Pure Land or Western Paradise. By the third century AD, in a second translation of the *Pure Land sutra,* Guanyin is promoted to being successor to Amitābha. In that same translation is the passage:

> 'If among mankind there be any worthy men or women who fall into terror of the officials, they have only to entrust themselves to these Bodhisattvas, Avālokiteśvara and Mahāsthāmaprāpta★, and they will assuredly be saved.'

★ Mahāsthāmaprāpta is the representation of the Buddha-wisdom of Amitābha, who stands to the Buddha's right, with Avālokiteśvara on the left. The two Bodhisattvas serve a dual function, complementing the central figure; together they are called the Three Holy Ones of the western region.

Such an admirably accomodating and merciful disposition confirmed the popularity of the Bodhisattva within the Chinese faith, and with the spread of Pure Land doctrines during the Tang dynasty (AD 618–906), Guanyin assumed an increasing independence and fame, with no less than 33 different forms recorded. From the middle of the Tang dynasty onwards, when Buddhism in China was suffering a very gradual but perceptible decline, the cult of Guanyin was strengthened by secular and magical powers attributed to the deity, so that by the tenth century the Bodhisattva Guanyin was probably the most popular figure in Chinese Buddhism. This syncretic popularisation, aided by the intellectual decline of Buddhism, caused Guanyin's appearance to alter during the succeeding Ming dynasty (1368–1644). Fusion with Chinese Taoist legends, and with the tutelary goddesses of popular religion, meant that Guanyin was then often portrayed in a female aspect.

The decrease in the power and influence of the Buddhist church in the Tang was caused by its inability to continue to attract large-scale Imperial patronage and revenue and by severe official persecution of Buddhism in the ninth century. However, the decline was halted and reversed during the Song period (960–1279), both by the Song rulers and by the invaders who wrested the northern provinces of China from Song rule. The Chinese Song state, founded after a time of great turbulence, never achieved the military strength of earlier dynasties and was constantly threatened across its northern borders by the 'barbarian menace'. The Khitan from southern Manchuria founded the Liao dynasty in the north, while to the northwest the Song were harassed by the Tangut tribes of Tibetans, who established a strong state in Gansu province and the Ordos region inside the northern loop of the Yellow River. In 1115 the Jurchen from northeastern Manchuria rebelled against the Liao and set up their own dynasty under the Chinese reign name of *Jin,* 'Golden'. By 1126 the Jin, in a series of battles with the ineffectual Song armies, had gained control over a large area of north China, including Shanxi province. (See Map 1)

The Jin rulers appear to have desired to adopt as far as they could the superior culture of the vanquished Chinese, including aspects of government, art and the Buddhist religion. Their conduct echoes that of earlier conquerors, like the Tuoba rulers of the Northern Wei dynasty, who during the fifth and sixth centuries were great promoters of

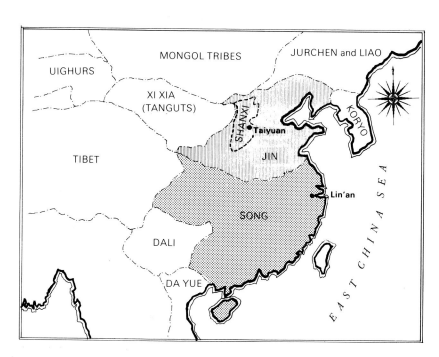

Map 1 China and surrounding states *c*.AD 1200, with the position of present-day Shanxi province.

Buddhist religion and art in north China. Similarly, the Jin stimulated the Buddhist church in the north, as is evidenced by the large number of Buddhist temples and images maintained during the twelfth and thirteenth centuries.

★   ★   ★

During the Tang dynasty strong cultural links had been forged with India. During the seventh century Chinese Buddhist pilgrims visited India, bringing back with them sacred texts and images. Foremost among them was Xuanzang, who was absent from China for sixteen years between 629 and 645. Indian monks and preachers returned down the Silk Route to China, and merchants travelling along the same road served to increase the flow of goods and ideas from India and Central Asia. Certain features of Tang Buddhist sculpture reflect a strong Indianising influence, chiefly to be seen in the postures of figures, and in their languorous, voluptuous beauty. After the fall of the Tang two main factors brought about a lessening of Indian influence.

In the first place, the presence of the Jurchen as rulers of north China, together with the activities of warlike peoples on her northwestern borders, caused trade along the southern branch of the Silk Route to diminish. Business continued at a sporadic rate, but the main arteries of communication with the west were by way of the sea route from south China to southern India, and overland via Yunnan and Burma to Assam. These latter routes of course facilitated trade between the Southern Song and her western neighbours, but did not greatly affect the condition of northern China. Secondly, Buddhism was in eclipse in the country of its origin and was rapidly losing ground before a resurgent Hinduism and an aggressive Islam. By the twelfth century the warriors of Islam had virtually wiped out Buddhism in India, and by the fifteenth century the entire Central Asian region had come under their sway. Thus although some Indian influence can still be discerned in Jin dynasty Buddhist sculpture, we must presume strong local elements.

The recognition of a so-called 'Shanxi style' in the painting and sculpture of this period was made by art historians earlier in the century. Among them was Osvald Sirén, who travelled and researched extensively in China and produced many books and articles illustrated with his own photographs. Laurence Sickman, who travelled in China in the 1930s, describes a number of temples in the valley of the Fen river, running south from Taiyuan in Shanxi. (See Map 2) Few western students have had the chance in recent years to renew acquaintance with these monuments, and although some sites, like the Huayan temple in Datong, have been refurbished, many may now be plundered of their contents, ruined, or put to secular use. When Sirén was travelling in the thirties he described how some buildings were boarded up to protect them from vandalism committed by local people, lately 'liberated' from the constraints and superstitions of Buddhist belief.

At the same time, large numbers of Buddhist sculptures and frescoes were being hacked out and transported to the cities for sale to Chinese and foreign collectors. The scale of this activity may be judged by the

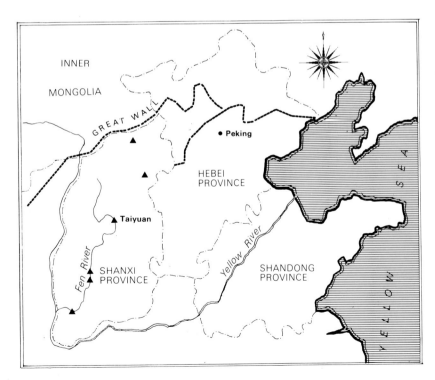

Map 2 Former Buddhist temple sites and the Fen River in Shanxi Province.

collection of one Paul Houo-Ming-Tse of Peking, which contained every sort of Chinese antiquity. In 1932 Paul Houo-Ming-Tse held a huge sale of some of these items at the Hotel Drouot in Paris, where no less than 38 large wooden sculptures were sold, the majority of them Song or Jin dynasty in date. If one multiplies this number by the total of collectors and dealers handling sculptures in those years, one may understand why many museum collections in America and in Europe contain fine wooden sculptures. Many must also be extant in private collection.

Several comparable wooden statues in collections in North America help to date the figure, and to establish its stylistic context. The standing Bodhisattva from the Nelson Gallery in Fig (1), which has been dated to c 1200 and is associated in style with the Shanxi 'school', may be compared with the Victoria and Albert Museum Guanyin. The features of the podgy, jowelled face and the sculpting of the stocky body are similar, as is the style and form of the clothing. An inscription contained within the figure tells us that the image, together with those of a Buddha and another Bodhisattva, were redecorated and repaired by one Feng Xiaoda, a temple artisan, on June (?) 10th, 1349. This date is approximately 150 years after the time when the figure was made. Such a detailed document might be supposed to chronicle the first major renovation. Thus we can gather some idea of the frequency with which wooden figures of this type would need to be refurbished. As a sculpture was repaired and repainted at regular intervals, each time in a manner fashionable at the period, or to the taste of the presiding abbot, it acquired many surface layers. The difficulty of tracing back through these layers may be imagined, and is chronicled in John Larson's account! It is also pertinent that the redecorations indicate that an image might change its appearance completely several times during its long existence.

Two large and similar Bodhisattvas, Guanyin and Mahāsthāmaprāpta (Dashizhi), formerly in a temple at Hongdong in Shanxi and now in the Royal Ontario Museum, are dated by inscription to 1195. Another link with Shanxi is provided by a seated figure in the Art Institute of Chicago. (Fig 2) This statue is said to have come from the Kaiyuan Temple near Taiyuan in Shanxi, and has certain features in common with the Victoria and Albert Museum Guanyin. A further sculpture which retains stylistic connections with the group is the standing Guanyin in the Metropolitan Museum of Art, which is dated by inscription to 1282. (Fig 3) This later date indicates a continuity of style in temple sculpture, which was maintained through the work of highly trained artisans. Inscriptions found on temple wall paintings and inside wooden figures make it clear that these craftsmen travelled about the country with their materials, models and copy-books, creating new images and repairing old ones.

Many of the Guanyin figures were similar in appearance to the Victoria and Albert Museum Bodhisattva, both when they were first

Fig 2 Bodhisattva, Jin dynasty, 12th–13th century. Courtesy of The Art Institute of Chicago.

Fig 3 Bodhisattva, Yuan dynasty, dated to 1282. Courtesy of the Metropolitan Museum of Art, New York.

painted and when they were subsequently renovated. The original decorative conception seems to have been a naturalistic one, for several of the figures were coloured pink in the flesh areas, with blue-black hair and red robes. Subsequent refurbishings in the Ming period appear to have favoured a gilded surface, and many of the robes, particularly the skirts of the dhotī, were embellished with raised floral and dragon *pastiglia* designs. Further repairs were carried out with the aid of paper binding on damaged areas, while the final surface on many figures is characterised by crude painting in harsh pigments. This last device may in many cases be the result of hurried repainting when the sculpture was about to be sold.

★   ★   ★

While the sculptural strength of the Victoria and Albert Museum's figure of Guanyin has always been apparent, some of the more delightful details have only emerged as the work of cleaning and conserving progresssed. Now we can see the subtle curve of the thigh, the folds of cloth tucked into the crease behind the knee, and the slight muscling in the smooth, round arms. Guanyin's 'cauliflower ears' have been cleaned out, while the modelling of his delicious swoops of hair and the intricate details of his jewellery and costume are revealed. Thus the slow, painstaking period of conservation work, besides leading to exciting scientific and historical discoveries, has also served to increase the beauty of the Bodhisattva.

Fig 5 Detail of flaking paint and paper on left knee.

The Sculpture before Conservation

In the text and captions all references to 'left' and 'right' in describing areas of the sculpture are taken from the observer's viewpoint.

Guanyin was withdrawn from exhibition in 1978, due to concern over the condition of the paint surface. Although the sculpture had been displayed in a glass case for many years, in conditions that were considered stable, the surface had continued to flake and the sculpture was becoming unsightly (see Figs 4 and 5). The sculpture had been in a private collection before it was acquired by the Museum in 1935, but nothing was known of its history prior to that date. Therefore we had no knowledge of any previous restorations that the sculpture might have undergone.

Once the sculpture had been removed to the Conservation Department we began our examination of the surface and initiated a photographic survey. Preliminary examination of the surface with a hand lens (x10) revealed that there were several layers of paint and gesso. The most significant fact to emerge from this examination was that the whole surface of the sculpture was covered with a thick fibrous paper, over which paint and gilding had been applied. Where the paper had flaked away one could see fragments of different colours suggesting that the sculpture had been restored several times in the past. The paper (which was as thick as all the previous paint layers together) was identified as the main cause of surface deterioration. Whilst reacting to small changes in temperature and relative humidity within the glass case, it curled away from the sculpture pulling with it the layers beneath. (See Fig 5)

The technique of applying paper to the surface of wooden sculpture to hide cracks in the wood and losses of the paint surface is a well-known Oriental technique. In this case the paper was about 1 mm thick and, although at the time of restoration the paper covering would have given an appearance of uniformity, it also served to obscure the finer carving, greatly reducing the delicacy of the surface detail.

In a great many areas of the Guanyin there was an encrustation of clay (2–3 mm thick). This we assumed, had gathered on the sculpture whilst it was in its original temple or shrine. It is possible, however, that the clay was added by a restorer or dealer in an attempt to 'antique' the sculpture. Clay is commonly found on oriental sculpture and usually results from genuine burial or exposure to wind blown particles in areas where the topsoil is easily eroded. In many cases these surface accretions are left on sculptures because collectors feel they enhance the feeling of age or 'patination' in the object. This is a romantic rather than a scholarly view and in fact often results in the true quality of the sculptured surface remaining obscured.

15

It is difficult to date accurately the clay and paper layers. If the clay accretions are genuine, then they must have accumulated whilst the sculpture was still in China and this (given the rather poor quality of the paint and gilding) would indicate a late 19th century or early 20th century dating for the restoration.

Although the examination of the sculpture at this stage had been very brief, one thing that was immediately apparent was the excellent condition of the wood. For a sculpture dating from the twelfth century the Guanyin showed remarkably little evidence of either mechanical or insect damage and only in one or two minor areas was there any sign of repair.

Methods of Examination

Our main problem in formulating a suitable approach to the detailed examination and treatment of the Guanyin was that we could find very little information on Chinese sculptures of a similar date or any publications relating to their conservation. Chinese publications are generally vague, regarding the history of carving techniques, pigments and mediums. A considerable number of papers on Japanese wood sculpture technique have been published, but these are not directly comparable and only provide broad analogies for interpretation.

Several museums in Europe and America were approached for conservation reports, photographs and technical data relating to sculptures of a similar type to our Guanyin. Unfortunately we found that although all the museums could supply some historical data and photographs none had detailed conservation or technical information.

Given the lack of existing reference material, around which we had hoped to build our research into the Guanyin, we conceived a basic programme of investigation which we felt would yield the maximum information. Not only were we bound by our ignorance of this type of sculpture but also by the restricted analytical facilities within the Museum. We were certain, however, that even with these limitations our combined understanding of the techniques of European and Japanese polychrome wood sculpture, would enable us to carry out a safe and useful investigation.

Our programme of investigation concentrated on two aspects of the sculpture:

(1) **Investigation of the wood structure**
   1 a   The method of construction and carving
   1 b   The origin of the wood
   1 c   Examination of restorations

(2) **Examination of the polychromy**

2 a   Investigation of the pigment and ground structure
2 b   Identification of the pigments
2 c   Examination of the overpaint layers

I   *Investigation of the Wood Structure*

I a   **The method of construction and carving**

From our research into other types of Far Eastern sculpture, we already knew that the basic approach of the Oriental sculptor to the problem of carving a sculpture out of wood, was very different from that of the European sculptor. The Oriental method is generally composite, joining together small blocks of wood to achieve the overall design of the figure. The European approach is, by comparison, much simpler and tends to make use of the single tree-trunk shape, resulting in upright figures of a columnar design.

There are two main reasons for this difference in approach. The first is aesthetic; the second is purely technical. Broadly speaking the figure sculpture of China, Japan and South-East Asia is dominated by Buddhist themes. These very often require figures such as the Buddha and some Bodhisattvas to appear in the Lotus position (see Fig 6) or other seated poses (Fig 4).

Fig 6 Seated Bodhisattva. Liao Dynasty, 907–1125. Shanxi Province.

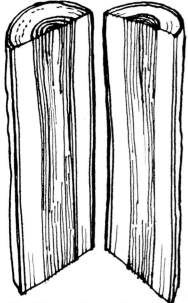

Fig 7 Diagram showing log split longitudinally. (Note the tight rings of the heartwood compared with those of the sapwood.)

In terms of composition, this demands a shape that is pyramidal in form which could not easily be fitted into the narrow dimensions of most tree trunks. Even in cases where standing figures are used, the fluttering scarves, draperies and mandolas require a broader format than that provided by a simple column shape. The complex figurative designs that were employed in 12th century Chinese and Japanese Buddhist sculpture, have no parallel in the Christian art of 12th century Europe. It is not until the fifteenth and sixteenth century in Europe that sculptural designs require the use of more complex arrangements of wooden blocks in order to accommodate flying draperies and outstretched limbs. The seated Madonnas and Crucifixes of Romanesque Europe do make use of simple composite systems, but these are really more akin to a puppet construction than the complexity of the Oriental system.

The main reason for using a composite block system is to overcome the tendency of wood to shrink once it is felled and begins to dry. The wood in the centre of the tree trunk (the heartwood) is much more compact and less prone to shrinkage than the outer layers (sapwood). If the sculptor divides his tree-trunk in two longitudinally (see Fig 7), in order to create two half round figures with flat backs, he will find that the tension between the heartwood and sapwood will produce deep cracks (or shakes) in the wood that could eventually ruin the work. European sculptors, when carving in wood, minimized this problem by hollowing the backs of their figures (see Fig 8) and removing the heartwood. Although this technique is generally effective, it is not uncommon to see standing Medieval sculptures with large vertical cracks in them.

If we compare these methods to those used by Japanese Medieval wood carvers, it will be seen that there is a very great difference in approach. A good example of these Japanese methods is illustrated by a seated wooden figure in the V & A museum (Figs 9, 10, 11). The method used in this figure is called the *warihagi* system. The sculptor constructs his figure out of several small blocks of wood each of which is hollowed, so that it is not only light, but the problem of shrinkage is virtually eliminated. Even in very small sculptures, such as this one, twelve or fourteen separate blocks of wood can be used and these are usually bonded together with a type of animal glue.

In Japanese wood sculpture the face is very often carved as a hollow mask so that realistic crystal eyes can be fitted into the back of the eye-socket. This example (Figs 10 and 11) uses two slivers of rock crystal to which two pieces of paper are attached. On these are painted brown irises and black pupils with a little touch of red at the corner of each eye. They are held in place by a pad of wool and a flat bar of wood fixed with three wooden pins. The wool is obviously used to cushion the brittle rock crystal from the pressure of the wooden bar.

Armed with the experience we had gained from the examination of several Japanese wooden sculptures and a certain amount of background research, we now felt that we should look at the construction of our

Fig 9

Fig 8

Fig 10

Fig 11

Fig 8 Back of 12th century Madonna showing the removal of the heartwood.
Fig 9 Japanese sculpture. (A.10–1967) Victoria and Albert Museum 15th–16th century.
H 38.5 cm. The sculpture has been constructed in 8 pieces of wood – the larger pieces
being individually hollowed.
Fig 10 Detail of Japanese sculpture. The eyes are inlaid and made of rock crystal lined
with painted paper to represent the iris.
Fig 11 Verso of Fig 10 showing the wool padding and wooden fixing behind the
rock crystal eyes.

Guanyin. There was evidence of several joints in the figure, although the
condition of the surface made these indistinct and difficult to interpret.
We decided that the only way that we would see the structure beneath
the paint and paper was by means of X-radiography.

Examination of the Sculpture by X-radiography

The complexity of the sculpture, and its fragility, meant that we could
only safely radiograph the sculpture from the front and the sides.
However we did take nineteen separate radiographs which gave us a
fairly comprehensive view of the internal structure of the sculpture. The
use of various angled views helped to identify certain shapes that
remained obscure when viewed only in profile. This proved particularly
useful when trying to differentiate between round dowels and square
dowels and the location of dowels within a block.

19

The radiographs made several things immediately clear:

a) That the Guanyin was made of many blocks of wood and that in some cases they were joined together by wooden dowels (Figs 12 & 13).

b) The sculpture itself did not appear to be hollow nor had the individual blocks used for construction been hollowed.

c) Several minor repairs seem to have been carried out on the sculpture. These were indicated by the obvious presence of machine made nails (Figs 13 & 14).

d) No signs of insect damage could be seen within the sculpture. Worm or beetle holes usually show very clearly in radiographs.

Although these facts could be immediately diagnosed from the radiographs, certain images remained elusive and difficult to interpret. For instance the frontal radiograph of the head (see Fig 15) showed a large rectangular shape, suggesting that a square-sectioned wooden block joined the head to the torso. When we looked at the side views of the head no trace of the block could be found. It was concluded, therefore, that either we were misreading the image and that it was not a three dimensional block but a section of the head itself, or, the radiograph was too dense and the block was not registering.

By placing the radiographs on a more high-powered light-box we found that there was in fact the faint outline of a block, although this was most clearly defined at the top of the block where a dark shadow appeared (like the one which appears above the block in Fig 15). This dark shadow represents an excavated hole in the head into which the block had been pushed, rather like a mortise and tenon joint.

In the case of the Japanese sculpture (Fig 9–11) the blocks were sufficiently small that dowels were not required for reinforcement. The much larger scale of the Guanyin meant that in certain areas, such as the limbs, head and torso, dowels were necessary to ensure strength.

Based on the evidence from the radiographs, we were able to establish the overall pattern of the wood construction (see Figs 16–19). This shows that 16 blocks were used to construct the figure and to construct the rock on which he sits. It should be pointed out that the rock is an independent element and the Guanyin is in no way joined to it. However, it is carefully shaped to accommodate the shape of his foot and the underside of his buttocks.

Although the main method of reinforcement in the sculpture is supplied by round wooden dowels, which might possibly be bamboo (see radiograph Fig 13), wooden pins are also used. One of these shows up clearly on the radiograph of the left arm (Fig 13) as a thin pale wedge connecting the arm to the knee. Another also appears at the front of the sculpture, fixing a section of the torso to the hips.

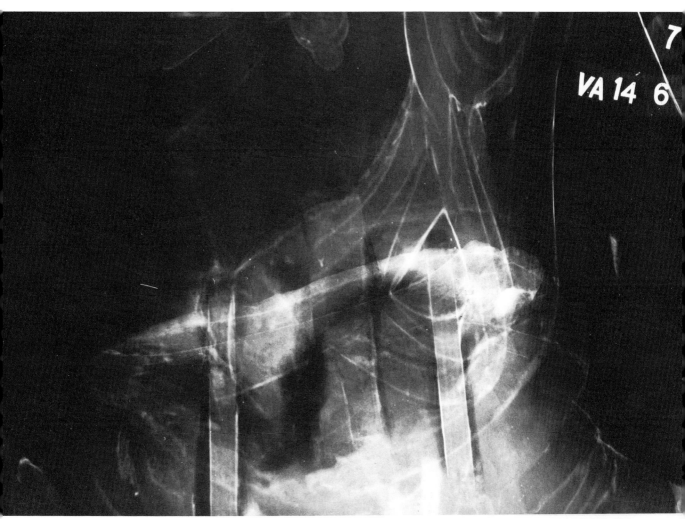

Fig 12 X-radiograph showing a cross-section through Guanyin's waist – the three vertical dowels joint the lower body to the torso – the dowels are possibly made of bamboo.

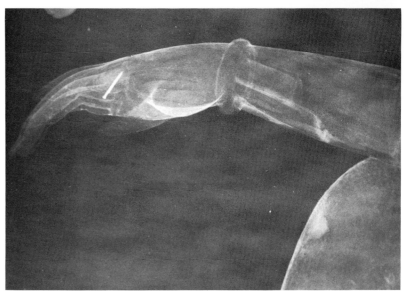

Fig 13 X-radiograph of left hand – the hand is dowelled into the wrist – a nail from a 20th century restoration can also be seen in the fingers.

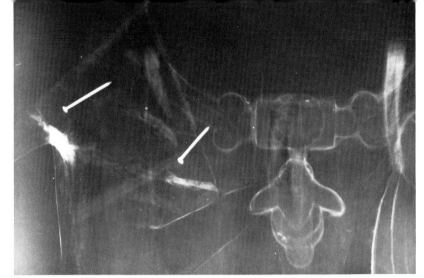

Fig 14 A great many machine-made nails were found when the sculpture was radiographed. All these are 19th–20th century in origin. The Ming restorers used wooden pins where necessary.

Fig 15 Radiograph of head. A large dowel or post appears in the centre of the head above which is a dark hollow area.

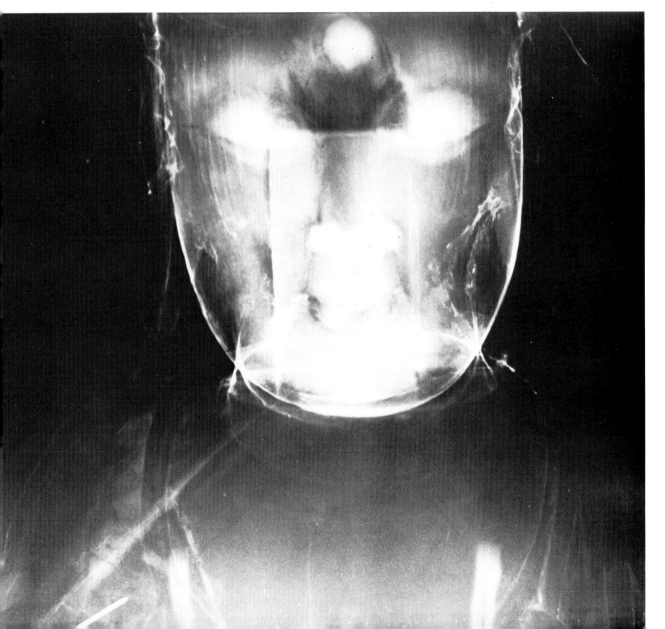

Fig 16 Construction diagram
Figs 16–19 Show the composite construction of the figure. Guanyin is composed of 12 blocks, the base of 4. There may still be other blocks concealed by dense layers of paint.

Fig 17 Construction diagram

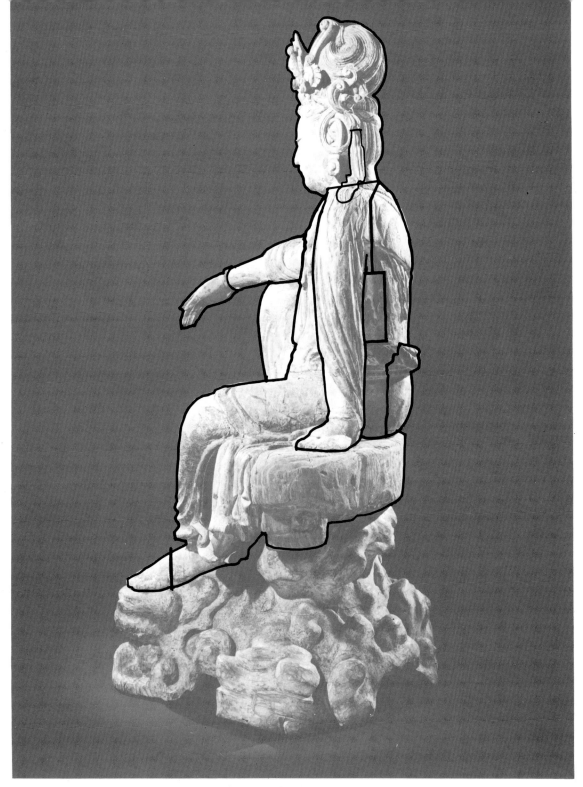

Fig 18 Construction diagram

Fig 19 Construction diagram

1 b Analysis of the wood

A small 5 mm chip of wood was removed from the underside of the Guanyin for analysis and identification. The sample was examined at the Jodrell Laboratory in the Royal Botanic Gardens, Kew. It was identified as Paulownia species, or the Foxglove Tree. It is found in Southern England but does not achieve the dimensions that it does in China where it grows to a height of 12 metres.

1 c Examination of restorations

The examination by radiography confirmed our earlier assessment that the sculpture had not in fact been subject to any large-scale structural restoration. The figures on the left hand had obviously been repaired, part of the right foot had been re-adhered, as had the lower part of the dhotī. Nails appeared in various parts of the sculpture (Fig 14). These were usually associated with seemingly original fragments of wood that had broken off and had been replaced in the very last phase of restoration.

Although at this stage we felt reasonably certain that the sculpture was mainly original, without removing some of the layers of overpaint we could not be certain that all the carving was contemporary. Any attempt to sample the wood in different areas would be foiled by the thickness of the paint and cause considerable damage. We felt sure that we would learn much more by studying the paint layers and evolving some scheme of chronology by which we could date the original and restored areas.

26

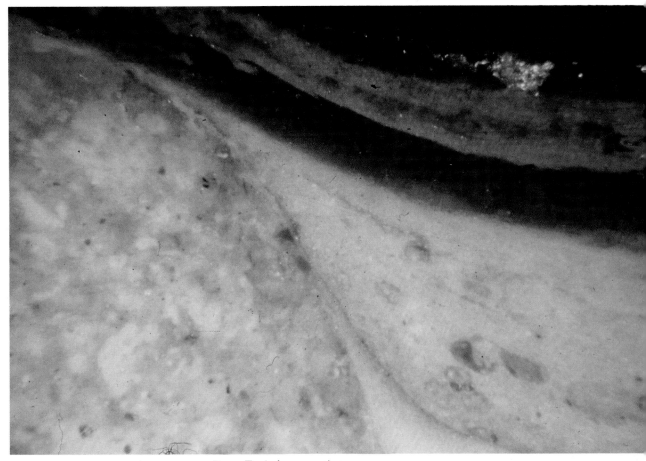

Fig 20 Typical cross-section

2　Examination of the Polychrome Decoration

2 a　Investigation of the pigment and ground structure

It was obvious from our cursory examination of Guanyin with a hand
lens (x10) that several layers of pigment and ground existed on top of the
wood. Before we could proceed with any cleaning of the pigment
layers, we needed to make some assessment of the number of layers, their
relative thickness and the quantity of surviving pigment at each layer.
To help clarify these points we undertook routine pigment analysis. This
involves the removal of tiny fragments of paint (usually less than 1 mm
across) from the surface of the sculpture. These are then set in blocks of
clear polyester embedding resin and polished to reveal the various layers
of gesso and pigment as clearly as geological strata. These cross-sections
are then examined under a microscope at high magnification
(x100–x175) and photographed (see Fig 20).

27

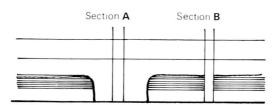

Fig 21 A section cut through the paint layers at point A would reveal two layers, at point B three layers would be uncovered.

After examining these cross-sections the analyst makes coloured drawings which help the conservator to interpret the structure and character of the various layers. These drawings act as a contour map by which the conservator can slowly build an impression of the layers that exist beneath the surface.

In all, some twenty-five pigment samples were taken. This meant that roughly three fragments were removed from individual areas, such as the face or the crown. In this way we could be more certain that the cross-sections we were obtaining were not revealing some uncharacteristic aspect of a specific layer. It must be admitted, however, that these cross-sections, because of their microscopic scale, are open to misinterpretation.

If the paint surface of a sculpture has been badly damaged in the past, when it is repainted the overpaint will fill in the missing sections of the original layer. In cross-sections (see Fig 21) where the scalpel cuts through at the wrong place (SECTION A) a very different view of the structure will result from that seen at the correct position (SECTION B). When relating the results of pigment analysis to the object under examination one has to consider these discrepancies, which are akin to those of the archaeologist digging trial trenches on an unknown site. The problem is particularly acute when the surface of a polychrome sculpture may have originally been patterned, which obviously produces cross-sections of considerable variation, in thickness as well as colour.

The conservator, when he begins the process of working down through the paint layers (with either solvents or scalpel) has to be very careful that he does not remove layers that are original. Very often he will come across discoloured varnishes or glazes that may look like later restorations but are in fact the remains of original surface treatments. This can often occur with red pigments where a very bright red is glazed over with a darker but more transparent red. These bright reds are often mistaken for an original treatment and the darker red glaze as a decayed varnish. This is not the case, however, for the bright red is merely a reflector to give depth and lustre to the darker red, very much like the medieval use of silver beneath red glass to simulate rubies.

It should also be remembered that artists and restorers change their minds. Although one would normally expect to find a single layer of pigment carefully chosen by the artist on any given area, in some cases the artist may have chosen to darken down a red that he felt was too

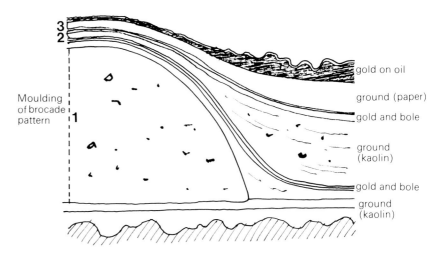

Fig 22 Cross-section (x175) showing pigment and ground structure on left knee.

Moulding of brocade pattern

gold on oil
ground (paper)
gold and bole
ground (kaolin)
gold and bole
ground (kaolin)

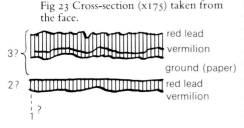

Fig 23 Cross-section (x175) taken from the face.

red lead
vermilion
ground (paper)
red lead
vermilion

bright in which case one would find a dark red layer that might appear to be an overprint of a later date.

The immediate results of our examination of the paint cross-sections were somewhat confusing. In some areas there seemed to be as many as twelve layers of pigment and ground, although some of these layers were so damaged that it was difficult to separate precisely the individual layers of restoration and original. In one particular area (the left knee) we did in fact receive a very clear result (Fig 22). This cross-section appeared to confirm that the raised gesso decoration in this area was original (ie was laid onto the wood) and that two successive restorations had taken place in this area. On the face (Fig 23) only two identifiable layers appeared, but in general, the cross-sections from the rest of the sculpture showed a consistent pattern of one original layer and two repaints.

2 b Identification of the pigments.

In these early stages of examination we had not attempted to identify the composition of all the pigments. Our concern was much more with the separation of original layers from restoration. From our brief examination of the cross-sections certain interesting features did emerge. In the first place the gesso was of a different composition from that used on Western painted wood sculpture. Secondly, some of the pigments used both in the original layer and the restorations were different from those used by European artists.

We first noticed that the gesso was of a different composition from the normal European gypsum and chalk grounds, when we wetted it with solvents. The darkening and the absorbency suggested that it was more akin to a clay. We thought that it might be a Kaolin for, on drying, it became very white. The National Gallery were later able to confirm by chemical analysis that the ground was in fact a Kaolin clay bound with an animal glue.

We found on the Guanyin that some of the colours were produced by the use of vegetable dyes rather than mineral pigments. For instance the hair (both originally and in later layers) was painted blue with an Indigo dye. In Europe at this period the use of Indigo would seem to be very limited, mineral blues being preferred. It is quite likely that the reasons for using a blue dye were primarily aesthetic rather than practical. Indigo is a rather transparent blue and when mixed with, or laid over, a black pigment (as in the hair of Guanyin) it produces a dark lustrous blue-black, that would be less effective if a denser pigment were used.

Some of the original layers of red were mixed with a lacquer medium as opposed to the size medium found in other areas. The red itself is quite possibly an example of Chinese Vermilion (which is found in Nature as a mineral, but which we know the Chinese produced artificially at an early date).

2 c   Examination of the overpaint layers.

The rather confusing results, that we had so far obtained from our analysis of the paint surface, could only be clarified by physical removal of some areas of overpaint. We began our test cleaning patches in the area of the left knee, because the cross-sections from this area (Fig 22) showed a remarkably consistent structure that was likely to yield positive information.

Before excavation of the paint layers began we had to establish the methods by which we would clean, consolidate and remove the various layers of pigment. One can see from photographs taken before conservation began (Figs 24–25) that it would be difficult to work on the paint without first consolidating it. We found that we could effect very good consolidation with a polyvinyl acetate resin (Rhodapas M) in a 5%–10% solution dissolved in equal parts of acetone and Cellosolve (2-ethoxy-ethanol). The particular consolidant has been in use at the V&A for over twenty years and its properties are well known. By using the Cellosolve, we found that not only did the consolidant dry slowly (which helps penetration) but it also softened and swelled the thick paper layer on the surface. In this way we were able to make the paint and gesso stick to the wood whilst making the paper sufficiently soft so that it could be peeled away safely from the paint and gilding beneath. Due to the thermoplastic properties of the resin we were able to iron down the paint flakes with a heated spatula, once the solution had hardened.

We were aware that the PVA solution was only a surface consolidant and would impart little more than a superficial consolidation to the wood. This did not concern us as we knew that the wood was in very good condition and the real problem lay with the securing of the polychrome surface. We also felt that it was unnecessary to impregnate the wood with a rigid synthetic resin that might cause damage at a future date. The Guanyin had been kept in a glass case for many years and had maintained a relatively stable condition. By removing overpaint, conserving the surface and keeping the sculpture in its glass case we felt that more drastic action would be unnecessary.

Fig 24 Detail of head before conservation.

Fig 25 Detail of knee before conservation.

31

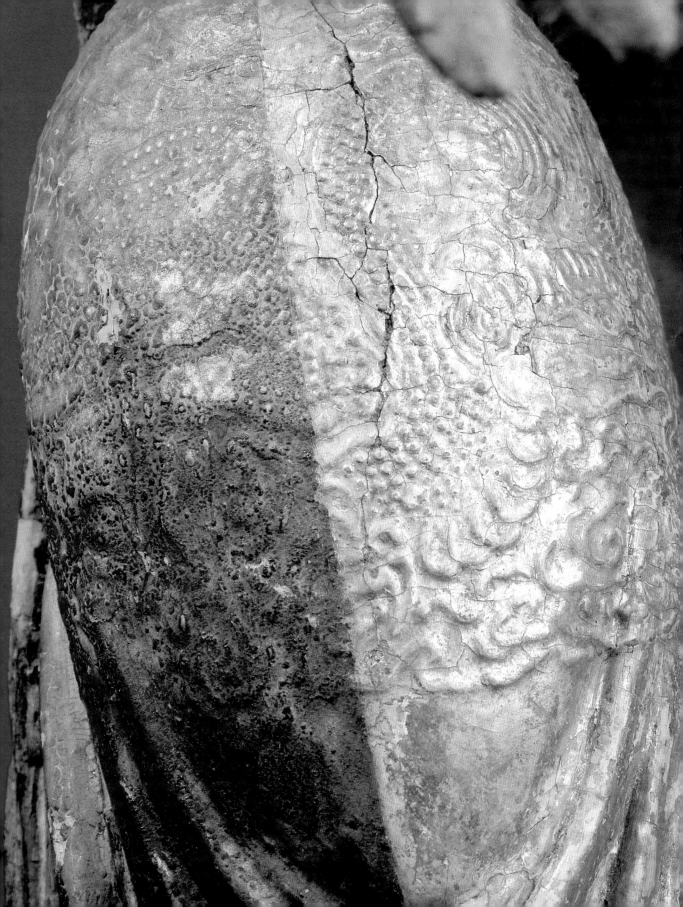

Conservation Policy

Now that we had some broad indications of the problems involved in the treatment of Guanyin, we could establish certain guidelines for the scope of our work. These, we knew, had to be flexible because we were sailing uncharted waters, but they were essential if our programme of work was to be coherent and structured.

a) From the very beginning it was agreed that we should keep a very detailed photographic record of all stages of the work. This was essential for our own evaluations of progress and would also serve as a record for future researches. The photographs were to be made both in black and white and colour. The inclusion of colour may seem obvious when recording a painted sculpture, but it should be remembered that some museums still only record their paintings in black and white.

b) The overall aim of the treatment was preservation rather than restoration. Although we wished to establish the original appearance of the sculpture in the 12th century, we in no way wished to restore it to that condition. To do so would be to ignore the changes that time had wrought in the sculpture and would also mean the loss of later restorations, that in themselves might throw light on subsequent changes in taste.

c) We wanted the processes that were in use to be as reversible as we could reasonably make them. Also, they were to be as discreet as possible so that they did not falsify or exaggerate the appearance of the sculpture.

d) It was obvious that the removal of overpaint layers would reduce the flaking of the polychrome surface, but we also realised that in removing overpaint we were destroying historical evidence. The original layers were still, of course, the most important ones. Against this, we did realise that in the future the study of various periods of restoration would not only throw light on the history of restoration techniques but they would also help to identify other sculptures of similar date. To this end it was decided that small areas of overpaint should be left on the sculpture at various points. We were aware that, if this method was insensitively applied, the surface would end up as a patchwork destroying the sculptural unity of the figure and detracting from its spiritual tranquillity.

Fig 26 Detail of left knee half cleaned. A layer of gold-leaf, oil and paper have been removed to reveal fine detail beneath, covered by delicate gilding.

Conservation of the Painted Surfaces

Now that the basic approach to the conservation had been established we felt sufficiently confident to undertake some preliminary test cleaning. The progress of our cleaning is laid out in Figs 27–30. In each selected area we would remove the top layer of dirt, pigment, gesso and paper and examine as much as possible of the paint layers beneath. In each case we would compare these findings with the pigment cross-sections and correct (or reinterpret) them accordingly.

SECTION A (The Right Knee)
In this area (see Figs 27–28) the crude oil gilding and thick paper could be easily parted from the much finer gilding beneath. The thickness of the layer we removed was about a 1 mm and one can see from photographs (Figs 26 & 31) that the loss of detail brought about by the application of the paper restoration was considerable. One could now see that the embossed decoration was a rather abstract version of the dragon and cloud motif, which is so common in Chinese art.

The most exciting result of our work in this area was that in removing the paper layer we uncovered some breaks in the gilded surface beneath. Through these gaps we were able to see some areas of bright red pigment and on one of these a fine gold line appeared (see Fig 32). Our original cross-sections (see Fig 22) had suggested that there were three distinct layers of painting but that all of them followed the same scheme. All layers were gilded and all of them were laid over the same embossed decoration.

The red and gold layer that we had now uncovered seemed to be completely different to the three known schemes. It appeared to be beneath the embossed decoration, and therefore followed the much simpler contours of the original wood carving. These suggested that there was a fourth (and possibly original) scheme of decoration and that it was of a much simpler design.

On the evidence of our investigations in this area we could now draw up a new cross-section of the pigment layers (see Fig 33). This of course did not mean that we would find a similar configuration in other areas (there might be three or five layers) but at least we would now be prepared to look beyond the levels established by the cross-sections.

SECTION B (Drapery over the Right Shoulder)
When the crude green overpaint in this area (see Fig 27) was removed a layer of gilding was revealed. The gilded layer was much damaged and in some places the green paint was only separated from the wood by a layer of paper and gesso. Although further tests with the scalpel suggested that as many as five distinct schemes might exist in this area, we could not as yet find all the colours indicated in the cross-sections (see Fig 34). We therefore decided to abandon our excavations in this area until we had more comparative information.

Fig 27 DIAGRAM 1 Overpaint layers.
The sculpture was cleaned area by area. The alphabetical order shows
the progress of the cleaning.

Fig 28 DIAGRAM II

Fig 29 DIAGRAM III

Fig 30 DIAGRAM IV

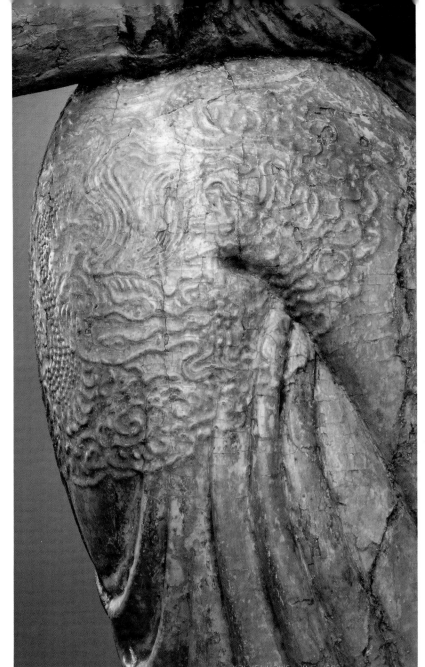

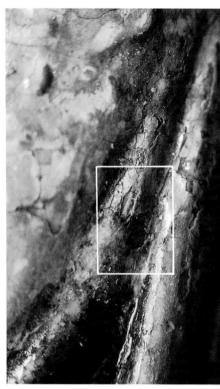

Fig 32 Detail of left knee. In an area where the gold and gesso had been lost, we caught our first glimpse of the red and gold decorative scheme that had eluded the pigment analysis.

Fig 31 The left knee after cleaning, showing the true quality of the gesso decoration. The pattern seems to represent a rather abstract form of 'Cloud and Dragon' design.

SECTION C (Drapery on Right Pectoral)

Beneath the red paint on the drapery we found the same thick layer of paper that we had encountered in SECTIONS A and B.

Below this we found gold bole and gesso, before coming to the wood (see Fig 35). Although our cross-sections had revealed that more layers existed, the remains in this area were so confused and fragmentary that we did not feel sufficiently confident to carry our exploration further.

Fig 33   Overpaint layers: see diagrams I, II, III, IV

A First area of cleaning – only one layer of restoration removed – see red area

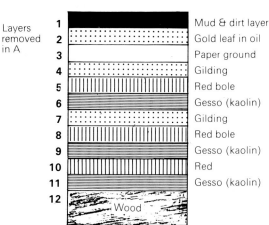

Layers removed in A

1 Mud & dirt layer
2 Gold leaf in oil
3 Paper ground
4 Gilding
5 Red bole
6 Gesso (kaolin)
7 Gilding
8 Red bole
9 Gesso (kaolin)
10 Red
11 Gesso (kaolin)
12 Wood

Fig 34   Drapes (green) on right shoulder

B The green overpaint was removed revealing gilding beneath – in some areas the gilding was missing and the green paint went directly onto paper or gesso.

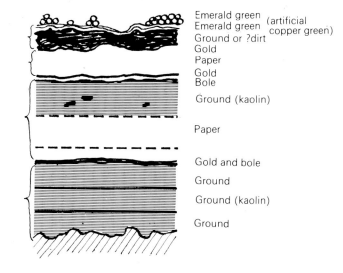

Emerald green (artificial copper green)
Emerald green
Ground or ?dirt
Gold
Paper
Gold
Bole
Ground (kaolin)
Paper
Gold and bole
Ground
Ground (kaolin)
Ground

Fig 35

C It was found that the red in this area overlaid a heavy paper identical to that in area A

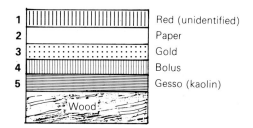

1 Red (unidentified)
2 Paper
3 Gold
4 Bolus
5 Gesso (kaolin)
Wood

Fig 36

D Flesh area – initial cleaning (not to the bottom layer of flesh colour discovered later

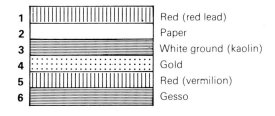

1 Red (red lead)
2 Paper
3 White ground (kaolin)
4 Gold
5 Red (vermilion)
6 Gesso

Fig 37

E The layers would suggest that the drapery was originally red and gold

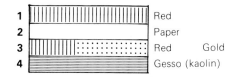

1 Red
2 Paper
3 Red   Gold
4 Gesso (kaolin)

Fig 38

F

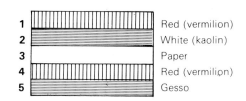

1 Red (vermilion)
2 White (kaolin)
3 Paper
4 Red (vermilion)
5 Gesso

SECTION D (Flesh area on Right of Torso)

On this part of the torso the paper layer was so thick that one could gain no sense of any specific anatomical form beneath. When we had removed three layers we discovered a thin film of gold leaf (see Fig 36). The gold was much rubbed and in general the bright red beneath it showed more strongly.

It was quite clear that the gold was not associated with the layers 1–3 (Fig 36) and that it represented a surface in its own right. By comparing the configuration of these layers with those in SECTION A, it now seemed reasonable to suppose that at one period the flesh areas had been gilded and that the bright red at layer 5 (Fig 36) was a priming for the gold and not a colour in its own right.

SECTION E (Draperies Mid-Torso)

This area was contiguous with SECTION C and generally followed the same pattern of layers encountered in C. One variation did occur which suggested that the velum of the drapery was treated in a different manner from the outside face of the drapery. Whereas in C the drapery had been all gold at layer (3) (see Fig 35), in E (see Fig 37) layer (3) was partly gold and partly red. This seemed to indicate that the mainly gold background was decorated with a red border or stripe.

SECTION F (Flesh and Drapery)

The flesh in this area (see Fig 38) was very damaged but in general it repeated the pattern found in SECTION D (see Fig 36). The drapery around the waist in this section retained very little in the way of pigment and did not show a structure similar to that in any other areas.

SECTION G (Neck and Chest)

The cleaning of this area proved to be very interesting. It not only provided us with considerable information regarding the changes that had taken place in the pigmentation of the flesh area, it also revealed much more of the original carved detail. One of the traditional attributes of a Bodhisattva in Buddhist sculpture are three rings around the neck (these are considered marks of beauty). In photographs taken before the cleaning (Fig 24) one can distinguish these rings but they are not clearly delineated. After the removal of the paper and some overpaint (Fig 40) the rings were very sharply defined.

Fig 39

G Cleaned further back than D to flesh colour

Fig 41

H

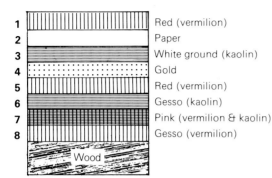

1	Red (vermilion)
2	Paper
3	White ground (kaolin)
4	Gold
5	Red (vermilion)
6	Gesso (kaolin)
7	Pink (vermilion & kaolin)
8	Gesso (vermilion)
	Wood

1	Yellow/pink
2	Paper
3	Pale gold
4	Gesso (kaolin)

The great revelation of this area, however, came when we found at layer (4) (see Fig 39) a virtually intact layer of gold over bright red similar to that found at layer (4) SECTION D (Fig 36). The colour of the gold layer around the neck was very different from that of the gilding on the lower torso. Instead of being a bright yellow-gold on bright red, it had the appearance of a copper-bronze.

Because the gilding was in very good condition, it has retained its original surface finish, whereas the more exposed areas of the torso had been extensively rubbed and damaged (Fig 40). The evidence provided by this area was crucial to our understanding of the appearance of the Guanyin at an important stage in its history. It was quite clear that at some time the flesh areas of the figure were carefully coloured to represent copper-bronze and that this was contemporary with the bright yellow gilding in SECTION A (see Fig 26).

We now felt that possibly the sculpture had originally been decorated with a fairly simple colour scheme and that at a later date it had been completely refurbished in a new and more elaborate style. The raised gesso decoration on the dhotī and the copper-bronze of the flesh suggested that the intention had been to make the Guanyin look like a copper-bronze sculpture that had been chased and gilded. This rather artificial style seemed out of keeping with the rather soft naturalistic style of the original wood carving and suggested that the new treatment originated at a much later date than the Jin period.

SECTION H (Lower Right Arm)

This area proved to be unlike other parts of the flesh in the configuration of its layers (see Fig 41). Layer (1) was a yellow-pink colour laid on to the usual paper priming. On all other areas of the sculpture the first layer was a red-pink.

At layer (3) (Fig 41) a pale gold layer was discovered that should have been contemporary with layer (4) in SECTION G and layer (4) in SECTION D but in fact it was totally different in character. The gold was not in leaf

Fig 40 Detail of chest with first layer of overpaint and paper removed. Remains of thin gold-leaf over a bright vermilion red can be seen.

form but a powdered gold which suggested that it might have been a later restoration and was not part of the overall scheme.

Many of the sections we had so far examined revealed contradictions in layer formation that pointed to a series of minor restorations alongside the major changes in the overall decorative scheme. It is quite possible that the different treatment of the right arm at layer (3) represents a localised restoration to a particularly damaged area.

SECTION I (Right Hand section of Dhotī)
The layers of pigment and ground in this area agreed completely with those found in SECTION A. Several traces of bright red identical to those at layer (10) in SECTION A (see Fig 33) were found. This confirmed our belief that all of the dhotī was originally of one colour and that the decoration was restricted to fine lines of gold highlighting.

SECTION J (Dhotī and Ribbons)
This area (see Fig 27) was very confusing. The red and green flowers on the white background seemed to be of later workmanship and contemporary with the crude gilding in SECTION A layer (2). The paint was on top of a very thick embossed layer (in places over 1 mm thick). It proved difficult to penetrate with a scalpel and there seemed little evidence of any paint layers beneath. The only area that did yield anything was the border of the overskirt; here, some gilding was uncovered, suggesting that there might have been a gold band at this point.

The poor condition of this section led us to abandon work on it, until we had more detailed information regarding the overall paint structure of the sculpture.

The blue ribbons on the figure's lap seemed to have only layers of blue and gesso on them. Cross-sections had indicated that there might be some gold on the ribbons, but we were unable to locate this.

SECTION K (Chest and Torso)
The flesh areas in this section (see Fig 27) are identical to those found in SECTION G (see Fig 40).

SECTION L (Hair and Crown)
The elaborate coils of hair on the head were almost completely covered with layers of mud and paper (see Fig 24 and Fig 42). During preliminary cleaning tests some of the mud was removed and an off–white layer was found on the hair. In other parts of the hair traces of black pigment were found on top of the white. Beneath the off-white layer we found the thick paper layer that seemed typical of the third or fourth layers on this sculpture. Beyond the paper the layers were somewhat erratic. Blue, in some places pale and in others almost black, appeared at various levels over damaged gesso layers. Our interpretation of the pigment structure on the hair after preliminary cleaning is shown in Fig 42.

Fig 42

I

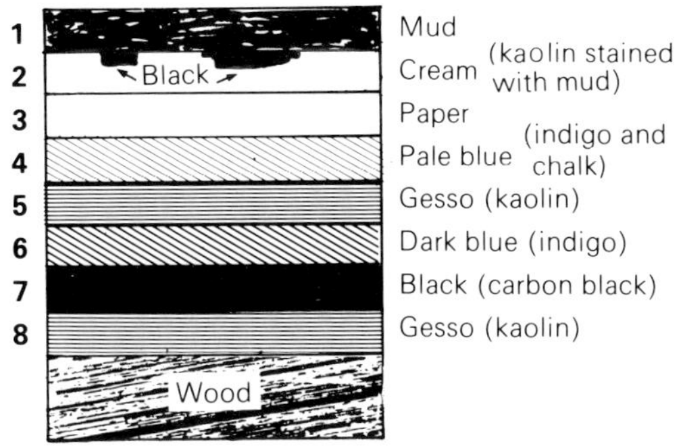

1 — Mud
2 — Black — Cream (kaolin stained with mud)
3 — Paper
4 — Pale blue (indigo and chalk)
5 — Gesso (kaolin)
6 — Dark blue (indigo)
7 — Black (carbon black)
8 — Gesso (kaolin)
Wood

Fig 43

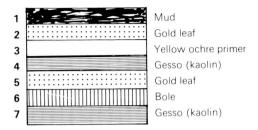

1 — Mud
2 — Gold leaf
3 — Yellow ochre primer
4 — Gesso (kaolin)
5 — Gold leaf
6 — Bole
7 — Gesso (kaolin)

The crown (see Fig 43) was covered, in part, with a thin layer of paper under gold. This paper was not as thick as the paper that covered the rest of the sculpture. However, it still seemed to be very fibrous and of an Oriental type. The paint layers on the crown appeared less complicated than those in other areas (see Fig 43). It does appear that the crown has always been gold.

SECTION M (The Face)

The face was the most damaged and inconsistent area so far encountered. The overall impression of colour on the surface was that of a strong red pigment over a white ground. There were many remnants of thick paper and, in some places, there were tiny traces of gilding over a bright red pigment, these would seem to be consistent with layer (4) SECTION G (see Fig 39). This would suggest that the face was also given the copper-bronze finish found on other areas of the flesh.

The greater part of the face seemed to be entirely without pigmentation and in many places only layers of gesso could be found. In all, only five distinct layers could be identified in this area (see Fig 44).

It was interesting that this had been the only flesh area in which we had encountered any traces of pink flesh colour at this stage. It was difficult to date this colour as it appeared at the surface and was not covered by other layers.

Fig 44

Section M

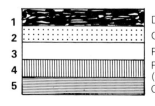

1 — Dirt/mud
2 — Gilding/pigment
3 — Paper
4 — Flesh pigment (kaolin & vermilion)
5 — Gesso

Fig 45

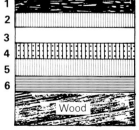

1 — Dirt layer
2 — Partial layer of pink over paper
3 — Paper
4 — Partial gold over red
5 — Pink red (vermilion & kaolin)
6 — Gesso
Wood

SECTION N (Left Ear)

In this area we came across a painting technique that had not been encountered on any other part of the sculpture. At layer (2) (see Fig 45) we found that two shades of pink had been used in the painting of the ear. The fact that the inner ear was a dark pink and the outer a light pink indicated an attempt at shading. This technique was again discovered at layer (4) where we found that the whole ear was painted bright red but only the outer sections of the ear were highlighted with thin gold leaf.

On further investigation we found that traces of bright pink flesh colour existed at layer (5).

SECTION O (The Necklace)

The top layer of gilding (see Fig 46) turned out to be identical to that found in area A (see Fig 33). It was a crude gilding over paper but beneath this there was a layer of red over gold. This gold (layer (4), Fig 46) was again laid on paper and beneath this another layer of gold appeared. This double use of paper again underlined the inconsistencies that had occurred in some cross-sections (eg SECTION H, Fig 41). It seemed clear to us that although there were probably three identifiable layers of restoration on top of the original paint, there had been at least two additional local restorations.

SECTION P (Right Arm)

In investigating the upper section of the arm we encountered the same pigment structure uncovered in SECTION H (Fig 41). However beyond layer (5) (see Fig 47) another five layers were discovered. At layer (6) (Fig 47) the fine, burnished gold over vermilion found at layer (4) SECTION G (see Fig 39) was uncovered.

When a large area of this layer was uncovered we found that a slight suggestion of musculature existed in the arm. The thick layers of overpaint had completely disguised the modelling of the arm so that it appeared as a simple round pillar without any indication of anatomy.

Fig 46

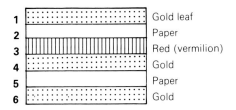

1	Gold leaf
2	Paper
3	Red (vermilion)
4	Gold
5	Paper
6	Gold

Fig 47

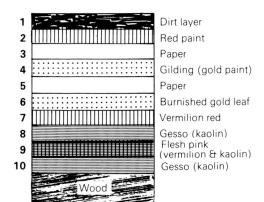

1	Dirt layer
2	Red paint
3	Paper
4	Gilding (gold paint)
5	Paper
6	Burnished gold leaf
7	Vermilion red
8	Gesso (kaolin)
9	Flesh pink (vermilion & kaolin)
10	Gesso (kaolin)
	Wood

Fig 48

Q

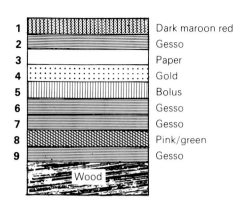

1	Dark maroon red
2	Gesso
3	Paper
4	Gold
5	Bolus
6	Gesso
7	Gesso
8	Pink/green
9	Gesso
	Wood

Fig 49

R See diagram II

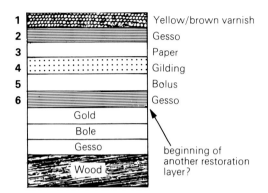

1	Yellow/brown varnish
2	Gesso
3	Paper
4	Gilding
5	Bolus
6	Gesso
	Gold
	Bole
	Gesso
	Wood

beginning of another restoration layer?

Although it would have been tempting to clean the arm back to the earliest layers, we realised that little extra definition of the musculature would be revealed, the thickness of the first five layers being twice that of the five layers beneath.

SECTION Q (Fold of Robe behind Left Knee)
Due to the poor condition of the paint in this area (see Figs 28 and 48) our investigations proved to be inconclusive. The character of the first seven layers (see Fig 48) suggested that there had been two repaints. Beneath this, however, at layer (8) we found a confusing mixture of pink and green paint. There was no evidence of a distinct pattern and the two colours seemed to exist on the same level, rather than one being on top of the other.

The two layers of gesso at layers (6) and (7) could be explained in different ways. Either the first application of gesso had not resulted in a uniform finish, or, the bottom layer of paint had already flaked and in some places the new gesso was laid directly on the old.

SECTION R (Drapery on Left Hip)
Beneath heavy layers of paper and overpaint in this area, only small traces of earlier decoration remained. From our investigations it would seem that originally this area was covered with a fine gilding at layer (7) (see Fig 49).

SECTION S (Rear Hip)
The examination of this area uncovered an interesting type of decoration that had not yet been found elsewhere on the sculpture. Beneath a rather jumbled mixture of fragmentary layers, a composite layer of green/dark-green/red/gold at layer (5) (see Fig 50) was discovered. This was all contained in a band some 6 cms wide (see Figs 51–52). The considerable remains of pigmentation suggested that

47

Fig 50
S See diagram II

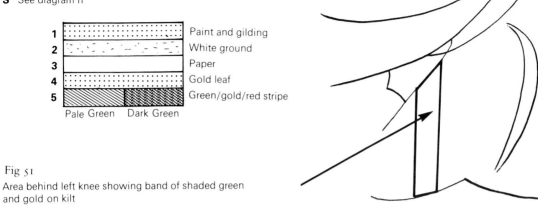

1	∷∷∷∷∷∷	Paint and gilding
2		White ground
3		Paper
4	∷∷∷∷∷∷	Gold leaf
5	//// ▨▨▨	Green/gold/red stripe
	Pale Green Dark Green	

Fig 51
Area behind left knee showing band of shaded green
and gold on kilt

Fig 52 Colour illustration of Fig 51.

48

Fig 53 Detail of Fig 52 showing remains of delicate painting.

the short skirt had at an early period been decorated with a deep border of green and that this had been edged with gold (see Fig 52).

The green band was very interesting because it contained both a light and a dark shade of green. This suggested a rather delicate form of shading and, in combination with the gold gave the effect of a shimmering silk. The subtlety of the original painting was further emphasised by the discovery, mid-way along the border of a circular medallion motif painted with great delicacy (see Fig 53).

The elegant richness of the decoration in this area seemed more in keeping with the elaborate decoration we had encountered at layer (4) SECTION A (see Figs 31 & 33) than that discovered at layer (10) in the same section. It reinforced our belief that the first major period of restoration was one in which the whole figure had been covered with various forms of gilding except for some small areas that had been painted such as the hair and certain decorative features.

Fig 54

T   See diagram IV   back of neck – top of shoulder

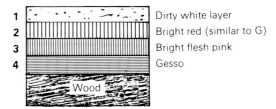

1   Dirty white layer
2   Bright red (similar to G)
3   Bright flesh pink
4   Gesso
Wood

On the back of the neck the paper layer does not appear on top of layer 1 – it only occurs on the front part of the neck – this suggests that when the sculpture was covered with paper the very back section of the figure was not covered.

Fig 55 Back of neck with original flesh pink pigmentation.

SECTION T (Back of the Neck)

After initial surface cleaning on the shoulder it was clear that the back of the sculpture had received very different treatment from the front. Halfway across the top of the shoulder the paper restoration ended and in fact only four layers of paint were found on top of the wood (see Fig 54). At layer (3) an area of bright flesh pink was uncovered which seemed extensive and quite complete (see Fig 55).

The fact that so few layers of restoration existed on the back indicated that the sculpture had been sited against a wall or in a niche and had not been moved during subsequent restorations. This is confirmed by the remains of two wooden inserts, or dowels, in the back of the sculpture (see Fig 56) which probably attached the figure to a background, possibly painted or gilded rocks.

In general it would seem that the back of the sculpture had undergone

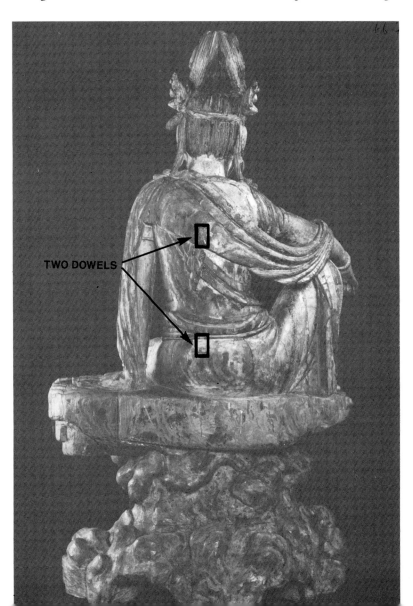

Fig 56 Back of the figure with two wooden dowels marked.

Fig 57

U See diagram IV   Base of hair at back of neck

Fig 58

V See diagram IV   Hair on back of head

1 — Dirty white overlay (paint)
2 — Blue/green (possibly yellowed
3 — Indigo Blue   varnish & blue)
4 — Gesso
   Wood

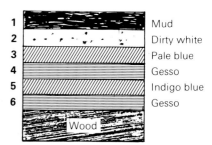

1 — Mud
2 — Dirty white
3 — Pale blue
4 — Gesso
5 — Indigo blue
6 — Gesso
   Wood

very little restoration and the only area to have suffered major re-painting was the hair.

SECTION U (Hair at Back of Neck)
In this area the layers were somewhat sparse and less complicated than those found in SECTION L (see Fig 42). Only four layers were uncovered (see Fig 57). This does suggest, however, that some attempt was made to 'tidy-up' the hair whenever the sculpture was repainted.

SECTION V (Hair on Back of Head)
The only difference between this area and SECTION U, was a coating of gesso beneath layer (3) (see Fig 58). This probably resulted from the restorer giving greater attention to this more visible area than he did to the less accessible area above the neck.

SECTION W (Scarf)
The scarf behind Guanyin (Figs 30 & 59) had been overpainted with a crude green copper pigment, which covered both the damaged and undamaged wooden surfaces. Beneath the green, an entirely different scheme was revealed (see Figs 60 & 61). In this scheme the scarf would have been black with an edging of gold leaf. As there is only one layer of restoration on the scarf and in general the back seems to have been untouched it would be natural to assume that the black and gold decoration is the original. However the character and quality of the decoration is reminiscent of that of layer (4) SECTION A (Fig 33) and at layer (4) SECTION G (Fig 39).

SECTION X (Scarf)
This area (Fig 27) hardly retained any fragments of pigment at all. On examination, the layers appeared different from those in SECTION W (see Figs 62 & 63). Instead of green over a black and gold layer, the green in this case covered a layer of gesso, gold, bole and gesso again before any black appeared. This suggested that the black and gold may well have been contemporary with layer (4) SECTION A, but the area had been so badly damaged that an intermediate restoration had been necessary. When compared (Fig 63) the sections show that three extra layers occur in SECTION X, showing that between the green scheme and the black and gold scheme, another scheme purely of gold intervened.

Fig 59 Crude green overpaint on scarf dating from the 19th century.

Fig 60 Painted scheme on scarf from an earlier period when the scarf was black with gold edging.

Fig 61

W See diagram IV   Scarf

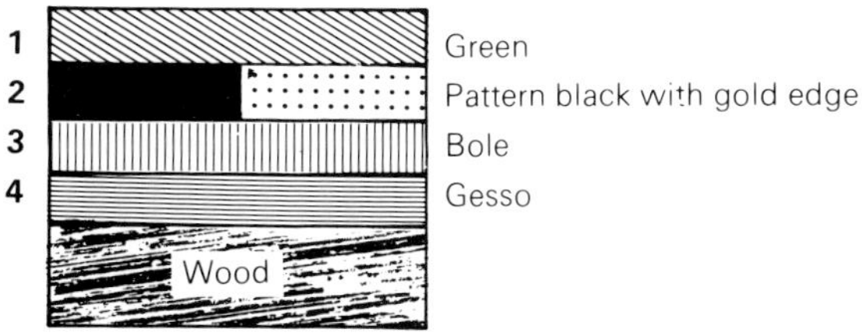

1   Green
2   Pattern black with gold edge
3   Bole
4   Gesso

Wood

The scarf would originally (at least contemporary with Ming restoration) seem to have been plain black with a gold edging. (This is not born out, however, by the layers in area X.)

Fig 62

X See diagram IV   Scarf

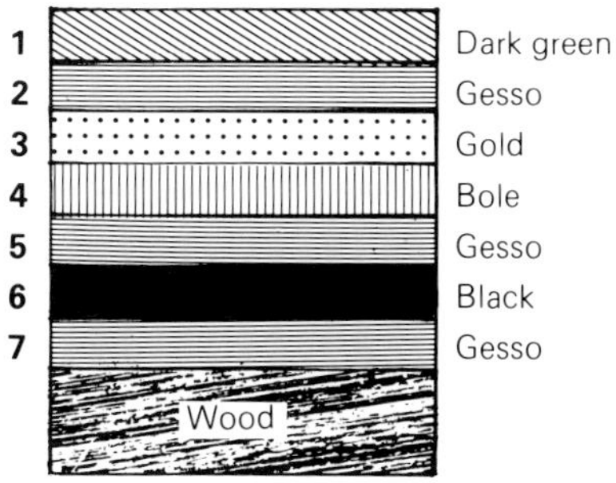

1   Dark green
2   Gesso
3   Gold
4   Bole
5   Gesso
6   Black
7   Gesso

Wood

Fig 63

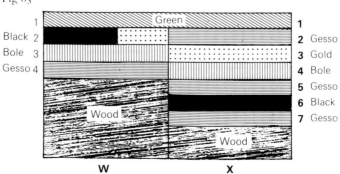

Black 2
Bole 3
Gesso 4

Green   1

Wood

1
2   Gesso
3   Gold
4   Bole
5   Gesso
6   Black
7   Gesso

Wood

W   X

Fig 64
Y See diagram IV   Hair back of head – above ribbon

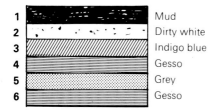

1	Mud
2	Dirty white
3	Indigo blue
4	Gesso
5	Grey
6	Gesso

Fig 65
Z See diagram I   Floral motif above right ear

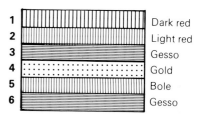

1	Dark red
2	Light red
3	Gesso
4	Gold
5	Bole
6	Gesso

Fig 66
A1 See diagram II   Front face of robe adjacent to Q

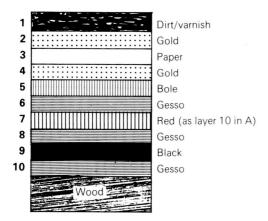

1	Dirt/varnish
2	Gold
3	Paper
4	Gold
5	Bole
6	Gesso
7	Red (as layer 10 in A)
8	Gesso
9	Black
10	Gesso
	Wood

Fig 67
B1 See diagram I

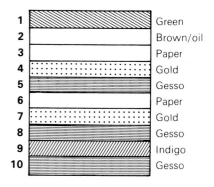

1	Green
2	Brown/oil
3	Paper
4	Gold
5	Gesso
6	Paper
7	Gold
8	Gesso
9	Indigo
10	Gesso

Fig 68
C1 See diagram II

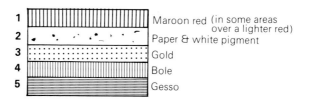

1	Maroon red (in some areas over a lighter red)
2	Paper & white pigment
3	Gold
4	Bole
5	Gesso

SECTION Y (Back of Head)

The examination of the hair in this section (Fig 64) revealed a pigment structure consistent with that found in the majority of similar areas. Three distinct phases of painting could again be identified.

a) Black over a dirty white. (This had occurred in SECTIONS Y, U and V, but only in small fragments.)
b) Indigo blue over a gesso.
c) Grey-blue over a gesso.

The paint cross-sections had generally shown a similar pattern, although somewhat confused and broken. Certainly the hair had always been blue, blue-black or blue-grey depending on the various mixtures of white or black pigment with indigo.

SECTION Z (Earring on Right Ear)

In this area no paper was found at any layer. During the last restoration of the sculpture this motif was painted with a dark red over the top of a lighter red. One might imagine that the dark red was a transparent glaze through which the lighter red would shine. However, in this case the dark red is too opaque (see Fig 65) and must represent a change of mind on the part of the restorer rather than a calculated effect.

Further examination (layer (4) Fig 65) revealed that this detail had once been gilded. From the lack of layers in this area it is quite likely that this gilding is either original or dates from the same period as layer (4) SECTION A (Fig 33).

SECTION A1 (Fold of Robe behind Left Knee)

The excavation of this fold (Fig 66) did help to confirm that there had been four different painted schemes on the Guanyin. This particular detail had originally been black, then red, gold and finally gold again.

SECTION B1 (Scarf on top of Right Shoulder)

The area adjacent to this section (SECTION B) had only five layers of paint, whereas the analyst's cross-sections (Fig 34) had suggested that as many as twelve layers might exist. We found that the remains of pigment at lower levels were so scarce that it was difficult to form any idea of the original appearance of this area.

We were able to confirm in our cleaning tests that a layer of indigo did exist at layer (9) (see Fig 67) as had appeared in the original cross-sections. It is possible that the indigo does represent an original treatment as there are three distinct repaints on top – two of gold and one of green.

SECTION C1 (Fold of Drapery on Left Thigh)

Only five layers were discovered in this area (Fig 68) with two distinct schemes of decoration, one red and one gold. It would be difficult to link the gold at layer (3) (Fig 68) with what was known of the earliest scheme. It seemed much more likely that it was part of the first or second restoration.

SECTION D1 (Right Thigh)

All that emerged from a more detailed examination of this area (after the investigation carried out in SECTION J (Fig 27) was that beneath the pattern of red and green flowers on a white background (see Fig 69) a fairly consistent layer of gold leaf could be identified. The raised floral pattern did not run beneath the gold layer and therefore must be considered an invention of the very last phase of restoration.

The depth of pigment in this area suggested that either this area had been gold in all previous schemes beneath layer (2) (Fig 69) or, that the damage was so complete that nothing remained of earlier pigmentation. It was felt that neither of these alternatives gave a satisfactory answer to the problems posed by this area.

A further investigation to a deeper level in SECTION J (Fig 70) gave a more acceptable result. This showed that the original paint layer was a bright green (layer (9) Fig 70). This was covered by two subsequent layers of gold and then the thick coating of raised floral decoration.

SECTION E1 (Drapery above Ribbons at Waist)

This area contained a form of painting that had not been encountered before, on this sculpture. At layer (4) (Fig 71) a fine clear red was discovered on top of a layer of gold leaf. There seemed little doubt that the red was intended to be a glaze and the gold leaf a reflector. This lustre effect was confined to the inner lining of the drapery and would seem to be contemporary with the scheme of decoration at layer (4) SECTION A (Fig 33).

Fig 69
D1 See diagram III

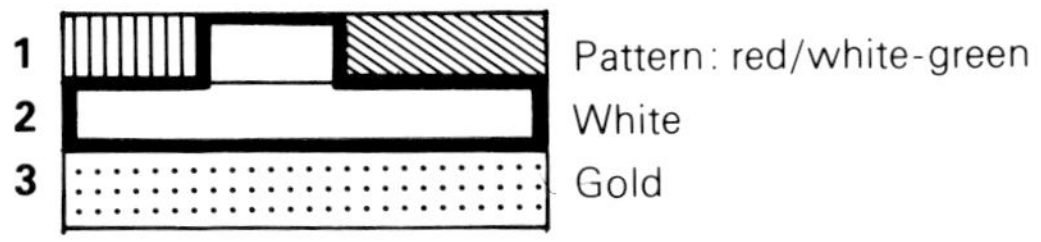

1	Pattern: red/white-green
2	White
3	Gold

Fig 70
J Appendix

1	1	Red & green flowers
	2	White
2	3	Gold leaf
	4	Bole
	5	Gesso
3	6	Gold
	7	Bole
	8	Gesso
4	9	Green
	10	Gesso

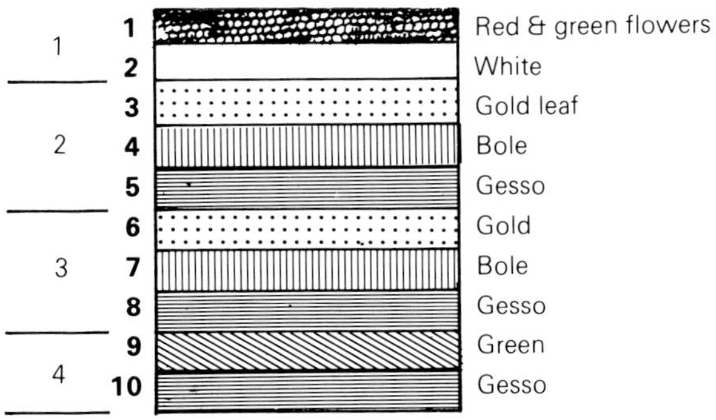

Fig 71
E1

1	Red
2	White
3	Paper
4	Red (glaze)
5	Gold
6	Gesso

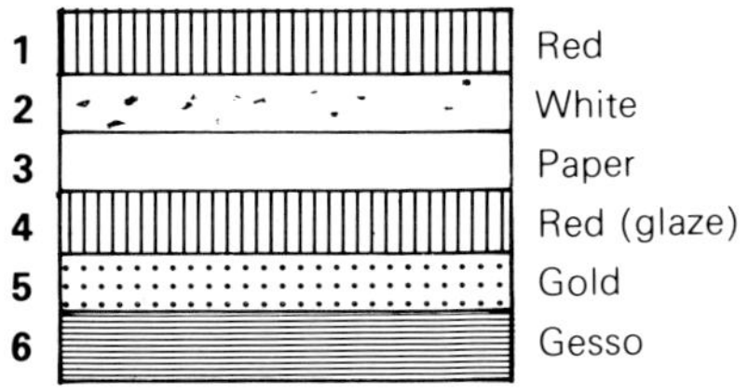

Chronology of Previous Restorations

The detailed examination of the pigment layers on Guanyin had given us an insight into some of the changes in taste that had occurred in Chinese sculpture during the past 700 years. Our evidence for those changes, so far, was confined to polychrome decoration. Now that we had laid bare larger areas of original (or at least, early) decoration, a more accurate assessment of the sculpture style could be made.

We had always been puzzled by the discrepancy in carving style of the two hands (Figs 72 and 73). The outstretched left hand (Fig 72) was distinctly elegant with thin tapering fingers and a very long fingernail on the smallest. The right hand (Fig 70) by contrast, was less elegant, being plump with straight fingers and short nails.

An obvious joint was visible on the left hand (Fig 72) and it had always been assumed that the fingers were a restoration. Our problem was that we did not know whether the fingers had been added at a later

Fig 72 Left hand (shown in reverse) – note the long fingernail on the little finger and the joint line across the knuckles.

Fig 73 Right hand showing the less elegant fingers without long fingernails.

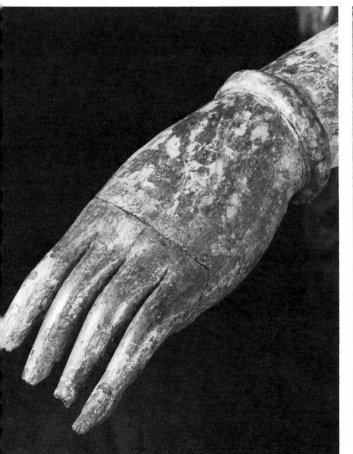

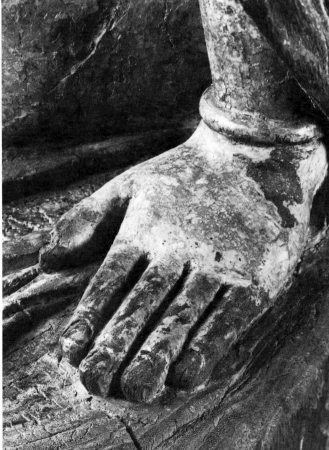

Fig 74 Detail of hand. The overpaint has been removed to show the paper layer. Under that the Ming painting scheme appears.

date, or, whether they were original fingers that had been re-adhered. Certainly, the style of the fingers did not conform with those on other sculptures of a similar style and provenance that we knew.

Although in Indian traditions a distinction is made between the use (and sometimes appearance) of the left and right hands, we did not feel in this case, that this was applicable to Guanyin. We could find no evidence that this was a tradition that obtained in either twelfth century Indian or Chinese sculpture. Also the pigment structure indicated that the fingers were of a later date. Beneath the overpaint (Fig 74) both the hand and the fingers had a uniform layer of gold over a red pigment identical to that on the other flesh areas (Fig 40). Under this layer, however, we found that the hand was covered with a pink flesh layer identical to that in Fig 55. The fingers did not have any layers beneath the red and gold and no traces of the pink flesh colour.

Although it would be possible to argue that the fingers could have been scrubbed clean before repainting, the evidence would seem to weigh heavily against this. The form of the fingers, the texture and colour of the wood, combined with the results of the pigment examination, confirmed in our mind that the fingers were not original and had been added later.

The stylistic differences in the carving and painting of the hands fitted nicely into a chronology of restoration that had begun to emerge during the examination of the pigment layers. All the earliest paint layers that we had identified in areas of original carving, shared a common feature in that they seemed to belong to a naturalistic scheme. The colours of the flesh, draperies and metal ornaments all indicated that the carving portrayed a human being dressed as a god, not the remote image that it was later to become.

On top of these early layers (which would seem to be of the Jin dynasty) a totally different scheme appears. It is a very elaborate and elegant style in which the sculpture is transformed into a simulation of a gilded bronze image with a surface treatment like that of chased and burnished metal. The damaged left hand was obviously restored at this time to fit in with the new decorative scheme.

A clear illustration of this change from the original scheme to the later one was revealed when we cut various 'windows' into the gilded area behind the left knee (Figs 75 and 76). We had been wary of removing restoration layers in this area, for, although we knew that traces of the Jin scheme remained, they were covered by a substantial layer of embossed and gilded gesso decoration which we could not remove without loss.

Throughout the process of cleaning and investigation we had formulated a conservation policy that we felt would produce the maximum information whilst preserving substantial remains of each layer of decoration. Although we would have liked to present the Guanyin as it looked when it was originally carved and painted, to do this we would have had to sacrifice the fine work of later periods. Being aware that methods of analysis are becoming ever more sophisticated we

Fig 75 After cleaning. The area behind the left knee was left to show the 4 phases of restoration.

Fig 76 Detail of left knee showing 4 phases of restoration.

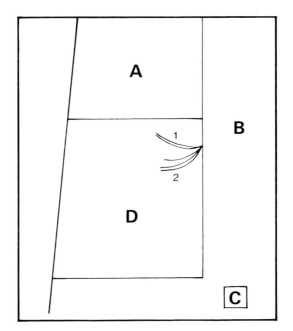

Fig 77 Diagram of 4 areas uncovered 1, 2, are remains of the Ming restorer's painted design for the gesso decoration.

felt that we should preserve as much material as possible for future investigation. We were certain that our current examination (although it had yielded much new information) was inadequate and would be improved by comparative examination at a later date.

In the area that we chose to penetrate to the earliest layer (Fig 76) it was possible to demonstrate clearly the changes brought about by the various phases of restoration. Four distinct layers were uncovered (Fig 77) one original, the three others, restorations. In area *A* (Fig 77) we have PERIOD 4 – this is the most recent and coarsest layer of painting. It consists of a very crude oil gilding over a thick Oriental paper.

Area *B* is a fine water gilding over bole and gesso. This represents PERIOD 3.

Area *C* is in fact identical to *B* and represents the decorative prototype for *B*. This section is identified as PERIOD 2.

Area *D* is the original Jin painting and is therefore identified as PERIOD 1. It consists of a layer of vermilion paint over gesso on which fine lines of gilded decoration appear.

To reveal the original appearance of PERIOD 1 we had to cut through a layer of gesso and overpaint nearly 2 mm thick, with fine surgical scalpels. In doing this we revealed a very interesting feature that gave us an insight into the working methods of the restorer of PERIOD 2. When cutting through the raised gesso decoration we found beneath the lines of decoration not only the expected red paint but on top of that some very fine black lines (Figs 76 and 77). We had found in the cross-sections made by the analyst that small fragments of carbon black had appeared in sections taken from this area. At that time we thought that they might be an original underdrawing similar to that found on panel paintings and frescoes. It was now obvious that we had uncovered a design drawn by the restorer of PERIOD 2 on top of the decaying Jin paintwork, as a guide for his new gesso decoration.

Unfortunately, although we had uncovered a fairly large area of the original red paint (Fig 76), there was no evidence of gold decoration such as that we had found in earlier tests (Fig 32). We decided to carry out an excavation in an area to the right of the right knee. Fortunately we were rewarded by finding a very complete area of original decoration (Fig 78) which showed clearly the gold line running along the top of a drapery fold.

Fig 78 Shows an area of red and gold drapery from the Jin period. Note the fine gold line running along the fold of drapery.

Fig 79 Reconstruction drawing showing the original naturalistic colour scheme used by the Jin artist.

Dating the Paint Layers

From our examination of the Guanyin we now had a reasonably clear impression of the appearance of the Guanyin at certain stages in its history. As a result of these investigations we were able to make coloured drawings reconstructing the various decorative schemes that had been applied to the surface (Figs 79–81). Although it was possible to isolate clearly the various schemes of decoration we had very little evidence for assigning a definite date to any of them.

Analysis of the pigments and the mediums, although it is interesting and will undoubtedly be helpful for dating in the future, is at present of little use for lack of similar comparative material. For the time being our only means of achieving any chronology at all is by means of stylistic comparisons with other sculptures, frescoes, bronzes, ceramics and textiles.

Fig 80 Reconstruction drawing showing the gilded bronze effect imposed by the Ming artist on the original scheme.

Fig 81 As Fig 4. Shows the sculpture with its 19th and 20th century restorations.

In her introduction Rose Kerr has outlined some of the stylistic comparisons that she considers relevant. On the basis of these comparisons we have drawn up a broad chronology that is laid out below.

PERIOD I	Jin Dynasty (Late 12th century) (1115–1234)
PERIOD II and PERIOD III	Ming Dynasty (1368–1644)
PERIOD IV	Late 19th–early 20th century

We have little doubt regarding the dating of the scheme in PERIOD I as there are many other examples of naturalistically painted Jin sculptures, with realistically carved anatomical details.

The dating of PERIODS II and III is rather vague but one could reasonably assume that the Guanyin was first restored in the late fourteenth or early fifteenth century. Stylistic comparisons may be made between the raised dragon roundels on the figure's knees and those on early Ming porcelain, although the correspondence is necessarily a broad one; we have already seen that other Jin wooden figures, needing periodic repairs, were redecorated during the fourteenth century. Guanyin was then re-restored (PERIOD III) about a hundred years later. The reason that we can say this is that similarities in technique and material between the schemes of PERIOD II and PERIOD III would imply that they occurred within a single phase of taste. Certainly the sculpture did not degrade seriously between PERIOD II & III and it is possible that the reason for restoration stemmed from a desire to keep the image looking like brightly gilt metal rather than a serious need for restoration.

The dating of PERIOD IV is based on the fact that the paint layers are associated with the use of machine made nails for repairs. This would therefore suggest that the date of the last layer is early twentieth century although it could be a little earlier. The use of coarsely ground pigments roughly applied would also seem to indicate a late date for this restoration and could possibly be a hasty restoration undertaken to make the sculpture suitable for sale.

Conclusion

Throughout our test cleaning and investigation of the pigment layers we had been careful to preserve the aesthetic unity of the sculpture. The more we worked on the sculpture the more we realised the damage (both aesthetic and physical) that the thick paper layer had created on the surface of the sculpture. We therefore felt justified in removing most of it and leaving only some samples for future study.

During the work we became increasingly aware that the remains of the Ming restorations would give us the most visually satisfactory results. We did not feel that we could justify returning the sculpture to its Jin layers as this would involve the complete destruction of the Ming layers and would also endanger the Jin scheme beneath. We therefore settled for the result that is illustrated in Figs 82–86, which at least reflects the scheme that existed in the Ming period.

At present the historical study of restoration techniques on sculpture is in its infancy and one can envisage a much greater interest in this field in the future. By preserving and recording restorations on sculptures we will not only be able to study changing aesthetic tastes, we can also learn more about the working techniques of Jin or Ming artists and this in turn will tell us more about their own original works, as well as their restorations.

Fig 82 After conservation – overall frontal view.

Fig 83 After conservation
– side view.

Fig 84 After conservation
– back view.

Overleaf Figs 85, 86 After
conservation – details of
head.

Fig 85

Fig 86

Fig 87 Guanyin (FE 6–1971). 13th century. Overall front view.

Fig 88 Guanyin (FE 6–1971). Back view.

Fig 89 Guanyin (FE 6–1971). Detail of head.

Appendix

Examination of a thirteenth century wooden figure of Guanyin (F.E.6 – 1971)

For the purposes of comparison we decided to examine a small wooden seated figure of Guanyin (Figs 87–89) which also belongs to the Museum's Far Eastern Department. Our examination concentrated on the polychrome decoration of the sculpture. In all twelve separate samples were taken from the following locations:

1. Blue hair besides left ear
2. Gold collar
3. Pink ear – left
4. Blue/green lower edge of collar and undercloak
5. Red upper cloak
6. Red ribbon, broken fragment on left shoulder
7. Blue/green undergarment to immediate right of 6
8. Flesh pink, neck below and behind right ear
9. Flesh pink, left ribs, back
10. Black/blue edge of cloak, shoulder, front
11. Gold headdress, left front
12. Blue garment, inside right wrist

There were extensive traces of paint on the sculpture and our examination revealed that the surface had not been overpainted. For us, the great interest in comparing this later figure with the earlier Guanyin was the basic conformity of the two colour schemes and in the use of similar pigments and grounds in both.

The ground

The ground, as with the 12th century Guanyin, is composed of Kaolin. All the samples have at least one and up to four layers of ground beneath them. The layers vary greatly in colour and in some cases the final coat of ground was used as an undercoat. In certain examples the layers are colourless, sometimes a pale cream shade, in others a medium brown colour and one had an admixture of carbon black and red iron oxide to make it a deep brown.

Pigment samples

1. *The hair* The ground on this area is the particularly dark one mentioned above. The paint layer consists of pure azurite; a thick layer of extremely coarsely ground brilliant blue particles. It is the thickness of the layer and the coarseness of the pigment particles which produce the brilliance of the blue. In Europe a similar method of enhancing the richness of the transparent blue azurite is effected by putting a priming coat of light blue or grey beneath it.

2. *Gold collar* The ground on this sample is a light brown (tea) colour. There is a thin light-red layer of 'bole' containing kaolin and vermilion and then gold leaf. One section shows the gilding overlapping a layer of red paint.

3   *Pink ear* The ground is light brown kaolin with a layer of pale pink paint containing vermilion and kaolin.

4   *Blue-green, lower edge of collar* There are two layers of ground on these sections, but the light brown lies under the medium brown on one and over it on another. Over the ground there seems to be an extremely thin black layer which may be ink. From these small samples it is not possible to tell if this is a drawn line or if it underlies all the green paint, and acts, as the dark brown does on 1, to intensify the green pigment which lies over it. This green pigment has not been identified but appears to be a synthetic copper green. The pigment particles are almost round and were probably precipitated. The colour is a light clear copper green. A soluble copper salt such as verdigris, may have been precipitated on to an insoluble translucent white material such as calcite. The material reacts strongly with HCl, confirming the presence of a carbonate.

5   *Red upper cloak* The ground is pale in colour and the pigment layer, a light red, contains vermilion and kaolin. There may be a slight trace of a glaze.

6   *Red ribbon on left shoulder* The ground is a pale cream colour. On this there is a thin layer of orange-red pigment that is red lead (confirmed). Over this is a thicker layer of pure vermilion giving a rich deep red colour. The red lead underpaint may have been used to intensify the colour.

7   *Blue-green undergarment* This section is identical to 4. There is the extremely thin black layer beneath the pigment. As it is unlikely that any drawing would have been found only on the two green samples this suggests that the black was deliberately applied under the green to darken it.

8   *Flesh pink neck* The ground can be seen as four distinct and varying layers, especially on 8A. The pigment (visible only on 8B) contains vermilion and kaolin.

9   *Flesh pink ribs* This section is identical to 8.

10 *Blue edge of cloak* No pigment layer could be seen on this section.

11 *Gold Crown* The light brown ground has a thin layer of kaolin and vermilion 'bole' over it and then gold leaf. It is difficult to tell if the gold was applied as leaf or as a paint. The surface is irregular and flaky and it will be necessary to examine it directly to determine this.

12 *Blue garment, right wrist* This section is similar to 1 but instead of the very dark ground it has the very pale, cream ground. There is then a layer of azurite of similar appearance to 1.

Conclusions

The colours used in the polychromy of the Buddha are obtained from only three pigments: azurite, vermilion and a copper green.

Different shades and intensities seem to have been obtained by using different underpaints, not by mixing pigments. The only mixture was that obtained with vermilion and kaolin to give a flesh pink and light red.

Bibliography

Osvald Siren, *Chinese Sculpture from the Fifth to the fourteenth Centuries*, 4 vols (London, 1925)

Laurence Sickman and Alexander Soper, *The Art and Architecture of China*, second edition (London, 1978)

William Watson, *Art of Dynastic China* (London, 1982)

Derek Gillman, 'A New Image in Chinese Buddhist Sculpture of the Tenth to Thirteenth Century'. *Transactions of the Oriental Ceramic Society*, 47, (1982–1983)

Yamasaki and K. Nishikawa, 'Polychromed sculptured in Japan', I.I.C. volume 15, no 4, 1970.

G. Gabbert and W. Lieb, 'On the use of a Gastro-fibrescope for reading inscriptions on the inside of Japanese sculptures', I.I.C. volume 15, no 4, 1970.

Index *Figures in italics refer to illustrations*

74